With Wolves

WWF
World Wildlife Fund

A royalty of between 7% and 10% of the estimated retail price
is received by WWF on all sales of this merchandise.

Printed in the USA

ISBN# 1-57081-869-X
First Edition 1995

Front Cover Photo: ©Jeff Foott

DAY DREAM
PUBLISHING INC.

WWF

World Wildlife Fund (WWF) is dedicated to protecting
endangered wildlife and wildlands around the world. Since its founding
in 1961, WWF has helped protect hundreds of plant and animal species
and preserve millions of acres of habitat on five continents.

Wolves capture the essence of our dwindling wilderness, as they require large
undeveloped expanses in order to survive. Protecting the few remaining areas that
still contain populations of wolves is crucial to maintaining our nation's
natural heritage and providing wilderness experiences for future generations.

WWF-U.S. and WWF-Canada are collaborating on the Endangered
Spaces Campaign, designed to identify the last and best areas of biological diversity
in the United States and Canada. Included in the plan are efforts to protect the habitat
of wolves, grizzly bears, and other forest carnivores in the Northern Rockies.

For more information, please write to:

World Wildlife Fund
1250 24th Street, N.W., Dept. ZBL7
Washington, D.C. 20037

If all the beasts were gone, men would die from great loneliness of spirit, since whatever happens to the beasts also happens to man. All things are connected. Whatever befalls the earth befalls the sons of the earth."

— Chief Seattle, 1835

uring the day, wolves are shy, and rarely permit an approach … but at night, they are so fearless as to come quite within the purlieus of the camp and there sit, a dozen together, and howl …"

—J.K. Townsend

How sad that man has never learned to live with the wolf!

I have seen them differing in color from an almost snowy whiteness to a dark brown or black …"

—Dr. F.V. Hayden

Anyone who has ever heard it when the land was covered with a blanket of snow and elusively lighted by shimmering moonlight, never will forget this strange, trembling wolf cry …

"I wish I could describe this howl … take a dozen railroad whistles, braid them together and then let one strand after another drop off, the last peal so frightfully piercing as to go through your heart and soul …"

—H.W. Shoemaker

*F*iercely loyal, intelligent, playful, cooperative—
many of the qualities we admire in wolves are
qualities we value in ourselves.

he elusive wolf … always seeks the most

hidden places in the wilderness in which

to make his den and raise his young …

$\mathcal{H}$is eyes generally appear sparkling;
and there is a wildness and a
fierceness in his looks."

—Samuel Williams

*L*ate at night and early in the morning,
they set up their howlings and call their
companies together—at night to hunt,
at morning to sleep."

—W. Wood

Early Anglo-Saxon heroes and kings—such as Beowulf—often added the prefix or suffix "wolf" to their names to denote their courage, tenacity, strength, and fighting ability: qualities associated with the wolf.

*T*he winter … was a celebrated winter of deep snow. The wolves … had a pleasant time of it. They played around over the snow and were bold and impudent."

—E. Duis

"*T*heir cunning has always been proverbial."

—McWhorter

"*The diversity of their size and color is quite remarkable, no two being quite alike.*"

—*Audubon*

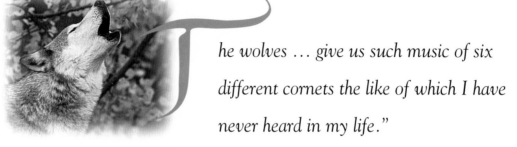

he wolves … give us such music of six different cornets the like of which I have never heard in my life."

—Henderson

espite legends and myths of "the lone wolf," wolves, like man, tend to be social animals, gregarious and close-knit as they follow the way of the pack.

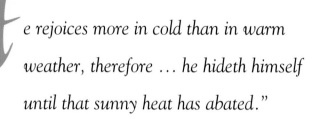

$\mathcal{H}$e rejoices more in cold than in warm weather, therefore … he hideth himself until that sunny heat has abated."

—Topsell

"Their gait is a long steady trot,

or quick and vigorous run."

—Dr. J.K. Barnes

"They go in droves by night, and hunt deer like hounds ..."

—M. Catesby

*M*an and wolf are the two most social of all terrestrial mammals. In wolves, family ties are valued above all.

*B*ig boned, lank paunched, deep breasted, having a thick neck and head, pricked ears … and a great bush tail."

—W. Wood

Elusive, intriguing, invisible even when they are nearby, wolves are secretive . . .

He is very bold, howleth fearfully, having fiery-flaming eyes."

—*Topsell*

 he wolf, like the bear, has been driven
into retirement, and is rarely seen in the
older settled parts of the country ..."

—Wailes

Native American hunters greatly respected other hunters—wolves, eagles, bears. The wolf was a great hunter whose strength and endurance they hoped to match.

"*A large whitish wolf made its appearance;*

then two more; their howls were answered

by others, until the gulches echoed ...

It was a moonless night, but the stars shone out ..."

—*Steele*